CALLED HOME

FINDING JOY IN LETTING GOD LEAD YOUR HOMESCHOOL
by Karen DeBeus

Preface

In November of 2011, I released my first ebook
<u>Simply Homeschool: Having Less Clutter and More
Joy in Your Homeschool</u>. The response was
humbling. I was thrilled that so many were blessed
by it. This summer I was convicted to write a book
to further encourage others, not to just rid
ourselves of distractions and simplify our lives and
homeschools, but to completely surrender our
homeschools to God and let Him lead us. I have seen
the fruits of this in my own homeschool and am
convinced it is necessary if we are to be truly
successful in our endeavors; not successful by the
world's standards, but by His.

God has blessed me with the desire and the passion
to encourage other homeschooling families. The
fact that I am able to do so is a true testament to the
power that can be unleashed in us if we surrender
our whole selves to him. May all Glory be to God for
all that He has done.

I want to above all thank Jesus Christ for dying for
me and saving me. I am nothing without this truth
being lived out each day. I want to thank my
husband whose unconditional support in all of my
endeavors is always present. To my children who
inspire me and give me hope for a future
generation. To my family who knows where we
have been and how far we have come. God is good.

Designed and Published by
FarmHaus Studios
All scripture taken from the NIV and ESV
Translations

Table of Contents

Appendix: 31 Days of Praying for Your Homeschool: Verses for the Homeschooling Family

Introduction

Once upon a time I was a scared mom preparing to send my first born to school. Then God stepped in. He changed my plans. He turned my world upside down. Even when it was the hardest, most frightening task I had ever faced, He worked. He led me to places I had never imagined with my family. Today, He continues to lead us. So often we resist and things are hard. Yet, when we surrender our plans, listen to Him, and let Him lead, there is peace. It is still hard at times, but with His strength and His leading, it becomes easier. There is joy in doing what He has called us to do.

> *"The LORD has done great things for us, and we are filled with joy."*
> *Psalm 126:3*

This fall I will embark on my seventh year of homeschooling. (Boy, I never thought I'd say those words...we started out trying it for *"just one year..."*) Maybe you are just starting out, or maybe you have been doing this awhile. Either way, there is most likely some amount of fear. Fear of the major responsibility that homeschooling is, or fear that you aren't doing it "right." Perhaps you are tired. Burnt out. Running on empty. Maybe you are up to your eyeballs in curriculum catalogs, reviews, planners, highlighters, label makers, and resources. Meanwhile the laundry calls, the dishes pile up, and the kids are tired. You are tired. You are trying to decide how on earth you are going to do it all. Or maybe you just are ready to throw in the towel all together.

Well, take a deep breath. Relax. The One who created the universe in a breath, the One who called you to this journey, is in control. Yes, He is in control of your homeschool. Is anything too hard for Him?

I often forget how small I am and how big God is. It is a funny thing how we think there is no way we can do it all- homeschool our children, be a mom, a wife, and perhaps work at home or even outside of the home. We think we need an extra clone of ourselves, or we just need to get a better system to organize it all. We forget we have the most powerful resource living right within us. His power.

> *"Now to him who is able to do immeasurably more than all we ask or imagine, according to his power that is at work within us..."*
> **Ephesians 3:20**

Chapter 1

THE CALLING

Jacob was a cheater, Peter had a temper, David had an affair, Noah got drunk, Jonah ran from God, Paul was a murderer, Gideon was insecure, Miriam was a gossip, Martha was a worrier, Thomas was a doubter, Sara was impatient, Elijah was moody, Moses stuttered, Abraham was old,... and Lazarus was dead. God doesn't call the qualified, He qualifies the CALLED!"
Author Unknown

Chapter 1
THE CALLING

If you are homeschooling it is because God called you here; and He doesn't plan on calling you here and then leaving you here alone. No, He walks beside you. He walks in front of you. He is leading the way.

> *"I have set the LORD continually before me;*
> *Because He is at my right hand, I will not be shaken."*
> **Psalm 16:8**

I never had any intention of homeschooling. It wasn't on my radar the year that my firstborn turned five. So you can imagine my confusion when I walked into the school building to register her for kindergarten, and I had a panic attack. All of a sudden I felt scared. I was shaking, sick to my stomach, and dizzy. I left the building in a daze. All I could think was, *"She is not going here."* I was so confused. Where did this come from? Was it just the jitters of sending a child off to school for the first time? Or was it something more?

As time went on, I knew it was something more. I knew that deep down God was calling me to something different. Everywhere I went I was seeing things about homeschooling, meeting people that homeschooled, or was reading about homeschooling. It was following me! God was chasing me, and I was running away from Him. (as fast as I could!)

There was no way I was going to homeschool. It seemed a big task, and I was not organized by nature. I was a messy little girl who was always losing things, forgetting things, and just plain disorganized. I never was a great student when I was young. I wasn't a certified "teacher." Even more though, I was worried about what people would think of me (yes, that ugly sin of pride.) What would our families think?

They were not happy. Even if I wanted to homeschool, I didn't think it was possible. There was serious opposition in my way without support from our families. I didn't want to cause conflict among the people I love or have people think I was just plain crazy. I saw homeschooling as an impossibility.

> *"For nothing is impossible with God."*
> **Luke 1:37**

Over that summer, the verses that continued to speak to me were the ones about pleasing God and not man. I knew that I could not worry about what anyone thought of me, but God. His was the only opinion that mattered. Even if I had no one left here on earth supporting me, if I pleased Him, then ultimately that is all that would matter.

Yet it is hard. We want to please our families. We want to please our loved ones and have their support and approval. We don't always want to stick out in a crowd as someone who is doing something "different." Yet I knew if I followed God and not man, He would take care of the rest. He promises that. He was in control and He would bless me for obedience.

> *"Am I now trying to win the approval of men, or of God?*
> *Or am I trying to please men?*
> *If I were still trying to please men,*
> *I would not be a servant of Christ."*
> *Galatians 1:10*

And He did. Boy, did He ever. I cannot even imagine what my life would be like if I had not obeyed the call. Our family has been blessed beyond measure by homeschooling. It is now a passion of mine. So even when I thought it was impossible, He not only made it possible, He made it surpass my wildest dreams. Isn't He wonderful?

My story is just that. My story. Everyone has a story. Each is unique in what He has done for us. Yet at the center of it all we share something. ***The calling.*** He has called us to this wonderful journey with our families. He has called us to educate our children at home, which as most of us know is about so much more than just educating them. It is a lifestyle, a way to disciple our children, and a treasure to spend those fleeting moments that pass much too quickly, with them.

So think back to when you first began homeschooling. Do you remember the fear? Or perhaps you were thrilled and excited? Or maybe you had no idea what you were getting yourself into (I sure didn't!) Yet, do you remember God calling you? Did you feel a pull? Were scriptures telling you this was your duty? Was God pointing you in this direction (or dragging you, like He did for me!)

It is so important to keep those days fresh in our minds and to remember why we are homeschooling. Often, once we get into the swing of things, we let all of the distractions pull at us and we quickly forget how we ended up here in the first place. **We are here because God called us here.** If you are on this journey, it is merely because He gave you the strength to take that first step.

Take a moment to pray about your goals for your homeschool. Remember why you are here and then ask God to direct your steps in the rest. Write it down. Then, claim a verse for your homeschool. Display it where you can see it easily during the day. Thank God for calling you here, and remember He is the reason you are here.

Another option is to write a mission statement for your homeschool. Then, take some time as a family to print it out, write it out, or however you want to creatively display it. Hang it in your home and let it be a reminder of why your family is homeschooling, and what your family's goals are for homeschooling. Each family has unique goals, and God has different plans for each family, but ultimately we all are here because He called us to this journey.

These visuals will help keep your focus on Him, especially on those days where you face difficulty. We actually wrote out our family mission statement on a day where we were all having a hard time. Attitudes were poor, mommy was tired, and everyone was snippy. There wasn't much motivation for schoolwork. I gathered everyone into our family room and we talked about why we homeschool. We talked about how God called us here and how we are going to continue on this journey as long as He continues to lead us. We then came up with a mission statements as a family, printed it out, and hung it on our family room wall. Now we have a constant visual reminder of why we are here.

We need to know that none of us are equipped for this task. Not one. That is the beauty of God's work. He calls us and then He equips us. You don't need to be organized, or a teacher, or perfect. No one is. He supplies exactly what we need to complete the tasks that we are given. If He called you to homeschool, He will equip you, but you must rely on Him and not on your own strength. Admit that you are not ultimately in charge.

God does not call the equipped, he equips the called

So many people tell me they could never homeschool. They say that they are not patient enough, disciplined enough, or smart enough. I say, *"Neither am I."* I never started this thinking, *"Oh yes,*

I am the perfect candidate for this. I am very organized, extremely patient with my kids, and will certainly be able to spend all day with them and not think it is difficult. I am extraordinarily disciplined and this will be so easy for me!" The truth is, God has supplied me with all that I need to be on this journey and to continue to press on.

Our kids are our ministry. Our homes are our mission field. Just like a missionary going into the jungle, it is hard. Do you think any missionary goes into their field thinking, *"This is so easy!"* No. Neither do we. God supplies missionaries with the strength they need, just as He supplies us, each and everyday, in the mission field that we call home.

Just like anyone is called to any mission in life, we are privileged to be called to educate our children at home. Yes, I said privileged. Even though it can be difficult, isn't that what God promises? He promises to work in the difficulty. When we trust, He works. He works beyond our strength and takes us to places we never could dream of on our own. Remember the calling; there is joy in answering the call.

Chapter 2

Don't Forget Who is Really in Charge

"He is the God of boundless resources. The only limit is in us. Our asking, our thinking, our praying are too small; our expectations are too limited. He is trying to lift us to a higher conception, and lure us on to a mightier expectation and appropriation. Oh, shall we put Him in derision? There is no limit to what we ask and expect of our glorious El-Shaddai; and there is but one measure here given for His blessing, and that is "according to the power that worketh in us." **A. B. Simpson**

Chapter 2
Don't Forget Who is Really in Charge

Once we lose sight of the fact that our homeschool doesn't really belong to us, and that we are actually not in control of it, we will suffer for it. When we try to do things in our own strength or because we think we can do it alone, we will fail. It is much harder to be in charge. So we need to remember who is really in charge of our homeschool. God is in charge.

When I first began homeschooling it was surely by divine grace. He called me to do the impossible and He provided the strength that I needed that first year. Yet, here is where the critical mistake was made. The first year went pretty smoothly, and it didn't actually seem so difficult (it was only kindergarten!) I did have the strength to homeschool. I was thinking, *"Wow, I am doing this! I can do it!"*

Nope. Wrong.

He was doing it all along. He was providing the strength. He was the one that had made the impossible, possible. Yet, I took my eyes off of Him and gave myself credit. Big mistake.

Then even worse, that summer we were about to embark on our second year of homeschooling. I was feeling quite confident with one year already complete, and started to think I could do even better. I started to become consumed with "stuff." I was consumed with catalogs, reviews, websites, curriculum fairs, etc. They all called me. There was so much to choose from!

The strong reliance I had on God to initially take the steps into this journey just one year before, was already fading. I was distracted by the now tangible things that I encountered in the homeschooling world. Everything seemed to tell me I could make our homeschool better. All I needed was "XYZ" and I would be more efficient, more organized, and successful. I floundered from one idea to the next. I read all of the information I could get my hands on.

Now, I am very grateful for the enormous amount of information that we have these days as homeschoolers. We are truly blessed to have an incredible amount of resources available to us at anytime. But it is a false sense of security. Beware. Are you forgetting who is in charge?

So often once we start homeschooling, we quickly become enthralled by all of the information out there. I know in the past few years the information has exploded even more than when I first began homeschooling. At our fingertips we can literally read about any and every program out there. The choices are endless. There is something for every learning style, every budget, and every family. We are so blessed to have so much available. Not only do we have amazing curriculum to choose from, we also have a huge network of support 24 hours a day and seven days a week. You can find any blog, forum, or group with friends ready to help you with any question you have, or when you just need a shoulder to cry on. I am grateful for that. We are blessed.

Then there is real life support. We have co-ops. We have outside activities. We have support groups. We have our network of friends that also homeschool. We are blessed.

Yet with so much, there is one major caution. Do not replace the One and only One that we need the most.

God.

He has called us here and He is able to do immeasurably more than we ask or imagine. He is in charge. He is the power source. The mere fact that I am writing this book is testimony that He does the impossible.

Let me explain. A few years into our homeschooling journey, I decided to keep a journal: a blog. I thought this would be a great way to 1) journal our homeschool year and 2) provide a way to witness to others, just what we were doing at home. There was still a tension in my family because I homeschooled, and I thought this was a non-confrontational way to show them what we were doing. I could say, "Hey check out our blog if you want to see what we do all day," without feeling like I always had to explain what our homeschool really looked like.

As I kept this journal I realized it renewed a love of writing that I had back when I was younger. Eventually I would find myself writing for a few other online contributor blogs, the first was **Heart of the Matter Online.** I gained more exposure for my own blog on there, and eventually changed the focus of my blog altogether to a blog about simplifying all areas of our lives and eliminating the things that distract us from God.

The blog's purpose was to teach people to have less {stuff} and do more {things.} I always had a desire to simplify and had written a few posts about it. Those posts struck a nerve. It seemed I wasn't the only one desiring a more simple life. In the homeschool community, especially, people were feeling bombarded with "stuff" and were looking to simplify homeschool. So, in the summer of 2010 **Simply Living...for Him** was born.

Then, in February 2011 I had the privilege to speak at the Heart of the Matter Online Conference about Simplifying Homeschool. The response was wonderful. Here was little 'ol me accidentally homeschooling, blogging, and now speaking about it. I had found my passion. I loved encouraging other homeschool moms in a real and authentic way. I loved connecting with others in the homeschool community.

The next fall I would turn my presentation from the Heart of the Matter Online Conference into a short ebook called **Simply Homeschool: Having Less Clutter and More Joy in Your Homeschool.** I felt led to do this by the Lord. I wasn't sure anybody would read it, but I did it anyway. I started selling it on my website, and much to my surprise people were buying it.

The funny thing is, looking back on when I wrote that book I have to chuckle at God's sense of humor. I composed much of that book while staying with my parents during a power outage at our home. We spent several days there and I was typing away much of the time. Here I was with the very people I was afraid of displeasing several years back because they disagreed with homeschooling, and I was writing a book about my journey. *In their home. With their approval.* God surely showed me that He paves the way when it is His will. He was making the once impossible, possible. It was a true testament to His power working in my life.

The book continued to sell on my site, and a few readers asked if it was available for the Kindle. I hadn't thought about that, but decided to give it a try. We made it available for the Kindle so that those few readers could read it, and at publication of this book, nine months later, it has remained a top seller at **Amazon.com**, often at #1 for homeschooling ebooks. No marketing plan. No publicity. Just my words and a heart to encourage.

At one point in the middle of all this I had a long talk with God. I knew I wanted to do whatever His will was for my ministry. I have always seen my blog as a ministry, and I wasn't sure about it being a "business." I decided to give some copies away. I truly wanted those that needed encouragement to have it. In a week's time I gave away over 2,000 copies. I still couldn't believe so many were interested in the book! My words were being used to encourage so many others and it truly humbled me and showed me the strength of my awesome God!

The reason I tell you all this is to give glory to God. Do you see what He does when we obey the call? He blesses our efforts. He knows my heart is to encourage others, and He has provided me ways to do so beyond my imagination or ability.

Now to him who is able to do immeasurably more than all we ask or imagine, according to his power that is at work within us,
Ephesians 3:20

Since then I have had the opportunity to speak at several homeschool groups, including my own state's convention this past spring. The most surreal feeling in the world was when I stood at the podium for the first time. Standing there I had a flashback of that scared mom just starting out homeschooling {me} sitting in that very audience several years back. I could barely catch my breath at the amazing work He has done in my life.

I was a messy little girl who could hardly keep my room straight. I was a lost teenager. I was a college girl living in darkness. I had been in the pit. Then He turned on the light and plucked me right out of the pit. If that wasn't enough, He called me to homeschool, which seemed an impossible task, and he continues to bless those endeavors. Nothing I do has anything to do with me. If you look back at my life none if it makes sense, but His plan always prevails. I give Him all the glory for anything I have done.

Psalm 40:2
He lifted me out of the slimy pit, out of the mud and mire; he set my feet on a rock and gave me a firm place to stand.
If He can take this messy little girl and work in my life, He can surely do the same for you.

I have done nothing on my own. He has been in charge the whole time. I just needed to take steps in faith and trust that His plans were better than mine. Once I realized that, it became much easier to homeschool. I knew that I had the Lord on my side. He had called me and He had led me here. He wouldn't leave me here to fail. It was all about Him.

Chapter 3

VINTAGE HOMESCHOOL

*"I will lead the blind by ways they have not known, along unfamiliar paths I will guide them; I will turn the darkness into light before them and make the rough places smooth. These are the things I will do; I will not forsake them.**Isaiah 42:16***

Chapter 3
VINTAGE HOMESCHOOL

Recently a friend and I had a discussion about a topic we coined "Vintage Homeschool." We were referring to the pioneer homeschoolers: those homeschoolers of 25 years ago that paved the way for us today. They didn't have the internet. They didn't have big homeschool conventions or curriculum fairs. They didn't have facebook or Pinterest. They may not even have known any other homeschoolers in their area! Can you imagine? I am sure they faced major opposition from their families and friends as well.

Yet, what they did have was all that they needed. God. Those homeschoolers had to fully rely on God in order to be successful. They had to remain in Him, commit their homeschools to prayer, and obey His call. They didn't have the extra distractions that we have calling us to make things bigger and better. They were just answering the call with God leading the way.

I can imagine the amount of prayer that went into those homeschools. I am sure embarking on such new territory was much more difficult than we have it today. There was no choice but to remain in constant prayer and focus on the Lord. They were truly answering the call, not knowing where it would lead.

As a result of those pioneer homeschoolers, we are here today. The homeschool movement has exploded because of their obedience and dedication to doing what God had called them to, and it continues to grow today. Those families persevered without homeschool conventions. They did it without the internet. They did it without support groups. They did it perhaps without many friends. They didn't rely on their own strength, but on His.

What if we did that today? What if we took some time and stopped researching every system out there? What if we put away the curriculum catalogs for a bit? What if we just steeped ourselves in His Word each day and covered our homeschools in prayer? Do we have any doubt that we wouldn't be successful purely in His strength?

I have done this at times. When I have felt like I am losing sight of the goals for my homeschool or losing sight of God's plan, I have taken a break. I have turned off the computer. I have stopped focusing on ways to improve, and just focused on God. I spent my time in the Word. Praying. I asked God to lead my homeschool and to supply all that I needed to be successful in His eyes.

If you feel that you are losing sight of Him or that you are starting to drown in your homeschool, take a break. Give yourself a week, or even a day, and just stop it all and surrender. Ask God to fill you with all that you need.

Unplug. Enjoy your kids. Snuggle up with books. The learning will come. These moments though will pass. Don't let them pass by with you being in a constant state of panic over doing homeschool "right." You will do it right if you are focused on God. Set your mind on things above and eternal.

Therefore, since we are surrounded by such a great cloud of witnesses, let us throw off everything that hinders and the sin that so easily entangles, and let us run with perseverance the race marked out for us.
Hebrews 12:1

Remember those who have walked this road before you. We are surrounded by a great cloud of witnesses, cheering us on through this journey. God called them. He calls you. Throw off those things that hinder and distract you, and walk ahead in trust and in confidence in His plan.

Chapter 4

DON'T SINK! KEEPING OUR EYES ON HIM

"Then Peter got down out of the boat, walked on the water ..."
Matthew 14:17

Chapter 4
DON'T SINK! KEEPING OUR EYES ON HIM

Let me take a moment to go back to my first year of homeschool. That summer I began to think this homeschooling thing was something I was doing by own strength. I researched every method, every style, and every kind of curriculum out there. I wanted to give my kids the best and everywhere I looked, another system promised the best.

That next year if things weren't going smoothly or we were having a bad day, instead of turning to Him, I turned to others. Maybe I could find advice from other homeschoolers-in person or online. I went to find solutions. I invested in planners, organization systems, and more books. If things weren't going smoothly, then I assumed we needed a new system or a different approach to planning.

So out with the old and in with a new. I was truly floundering. Going from one idea to the next was my new "system." I was always thinking, *"If I could just get things more organized, it will be smoother..."* I thought if I could just find a better "system" then we would get on track.

Truth is, it is not about the "system." It is about our hearts. Are we fully committed to the Lord's plans or are we constantly making our own plans? Are we always searching? Worse yet, searching outside of Him?

I was completely forgetting to stop, and focus on my children's hearts. On my own heart. I needed to go the Bible and seek God's instruction for raising my children.

Once we take our eyes off of God and His plan, we will flounder and eventually sink. Worse, we can drown. I love the Bible passage about Peter walking on the water. This is a perfect illustration of what happens to us when we take our eyes off of Him…

"Shortly before dawn Jesus went out to them, walking on the lake. When the disciples saw him walking on the lake, they were terrified. "It's a ghost," they said, and cried out in fear.
But Jesus immediately said to them: "Take courage! It is I. Don't be afraid."
"Lord, if it's you," Peter replied, "tell me to come to you on the water."
"Come," he said.
Then Peter got down out of the boat, walked on the water and came toward Jesus. But when he saw the wind, he was afraid and, beginning to sink, cried out, "Lord, save me!"
Immediately Jesus reached out his hand and caught him. "You of little faith," he said, "why did you doubt?"
And when they climbed into the boat, the wind died down."

Matthew 14:15-32

So here I was in my first few years of
homeschooling and I was screaming out, *"Lord save
me!"* I was starting to feel like I was drowning. I was
questioning myself because the abundance of
information led me to feel inadequate. I was
comparing myself to others, and I was floundering. I
even went to look at a local Christian school during
this time. I was starting to doubt myself. I looked at
how others were doing homeschool, I became
overwhelmed at the daily task of homeschooling
and planning homeschooling. I was consumed with
wanting to do it better. I felt like I was drowning. My
eyes were off of Him.

Interestingly enough, the verses immediately before
Peter walks on the water, tell the story of Jesus
feeding the 5,000. Imagine, seeing Jesus perform
this miracle, and how quickly it was forgotten.
When Peter began to walk on water, imagine his
surprise that He was actually doing it! Yet it was not
by his strength, but by the Lord's. He was walking
on water. The impossible was made possible.
Then the winds came. Just like in our homeschool-
things start to get difficult, a storm comes, and we
see the wind and we become afraid. Peter was
afraid of the wind. Or maybe he was startled. Maybe
he was startled by the fact that even though he was
walking on water through God's strength, there still
was trouble around him. Or perhaps his fear took
him off guard. Regardless, he did take his eyes off of
Jesus.

And he sank.

Yet, here is the beauty of this story. Jesus did not leave him there in the water to drown. Jesus and Peter both returned to the boat, and the wind died down. Jesus knows we will stumble and take our eyes off of Him at times. Yet He continues to be there. He does not leave us alone in the water.

So like Peter, I took my eyes off of Jesus in my homeschool. So many of us do that in homeschooling. I was like the Israelites. I was supplied provision from Him, and then how quickly I forgot what God had done for me just one year earlier. He had made the impossible {in my eyes} possible. He had provided the strength for me to embark on this journey. He had kept His promises. I had obeyed the call and He had provided.
How could I forget so quickly?

Yet, very quickly I forgot Him. I replaced Him with the world's view of success, thinking my success would come from the tangible. No. My success would only come from seeking the eternal, and seeking Him. God called me to homeschool and I quickly forgot I was doing it in His strength. Imagine how far Peter could have walked on that water if He had not feared when the first wind came. Imagine how far *we* could go if we keep our eyes on Him, *especially when the wind comes.*
What is making you sink? It is different for all of us. Some of us just don't feel equipped for this task.

Many of us face opposition from husbands, family members, or even our children. Are the days long? Are you floundering each day? Are you walking on water or are you sinking?

Homeschooling is unique in that it is always there; meaning we work in our homes as teachers, yet we are also managing our home, being a wife, friend, daughter, mother...the list goes on and on. We juggle many roles. There isn't much down time in the homeschooling lifestyle because our work is truly our life.

Yet, when we feel like we can't read another story, do another math problem, or solve another sibling argument, stop. Pray. Remember that you *can* do all things through Christ who strengthens you. That is not just a nice phrase. **It is God's Word. He says it and He means it. Believe it.**

Focus on the here and now. I have often joked that I can not read through *Frog and Toad* another time; listening painfully to each word being sounded out ever so slowly after teaching three children to read...it's tiring! Then thinking ahead that I still have another who will read *Frog and Toad* to me one day- it is daunting. Yet when I focus on the moment and the things that God has provided me this moment, it is doable. I see my children's smiles. I see their excitement over accomplishments, and I am reminded to take it one step at a time, and to enjoy even Frog and Toad.

As homeschooling moms it becomes much too easy to get caught up in the wind. We look at everything that is going on around us, and we begin to sink. We need to keep our eyes on Him, for He is the only One that can supply for our needs. We need to stop chasing the things of this world, and start chasing Him. The joy comes from chasing Him knowing you are fulfilling the calling and walking the journey that He has planned for you.

Chapter 5

REALIZING THE TRUE GOALS

"He that has trained his children for heaven, rather than for earth- for God, rather than for man- he is the parent that will be wise."
-J.C. Ryle

Chapter 5
Realizing the True Goals

So now we ask the question, just what is success defined for as a homeschooler? This is something that as a family, each person must define for themselves. I would venture to say though, that for most of us, success in our homeschools will be defined by the fruit that we bear spiritually.

Do I want my child to ultimately be educated or to be discipled? Is it more important for them to be successful financially or spiritually? Do I want them to love the Lord with all their heart, mind and soul? What will make me feel as though I have succeeded in this calling? Why did God ultimately place us on this journey in the first place?

These are all very important questions to be addressed. I fully believe if you are homeschooling it is because God has called you to homeschool. And if He has called you to homeschool, then your ultimate goal should be to raise children who love Him above all. To disciple children who truly understand what it is to love the Lord with all your heart, mind, and soul. Our goal in homeschooling is to bring God glory and to teach our children about Him.

If God chooses to have my children become CEOs or to become missionaries, then He will see it through.

My job is to seek Him. Obey Him. His plans will unfold for my children, and those plans may be very different from my dreams for them. Ultimately I have to let my children be the person that God called them to be. Not who I want them to be. Not to be like the person down the street. But to be the person that God calls them to be.

We can get so caught up in the academics that we lose sight of our true purpose. Of course academics are important, but I would rather my children know the Lord above all else and live for Him, than to be able to compute any difficult mathematical problem. I trust that if He wants them to use their gifts and abilities for big academic purposes, He will make that happen. I also trust if He has plans for them that don't include big academic purposes, then He knows best. Seek Him, and He will make known what His plans are for our children.

> *"In his heart a man plans his course,*
> *but the LORD determines his steps."*
> *Proverbs 16:9*

God has called us to homeschool so that we can raise up the next generation to be a godly generation. If we are not clear on the ultimate goal of this journey, then it is more difficult to stay focused. We will too easily get distracted. For instance, when we are floundering over what math program to use, and we spend countless hours researching. Stop and remember the goal. Are we focused on raising godly children, trusting God's plan for their lives, or are we placing so much emphasis on the perfect math program, that we have forgotten to be in the Word today, pray as a family, and ask God to lead us?

Are we focused on how our homeschool looks? I often get worried about the amount of emphasis we can put on our homeschool rooms or how things look. **God doesn't care what our homeschool looks like.** He cares about what our hearts look like. He cares about what our children's hearts look like. Don't spend countless hours on making things look "just so." Spend countless hours with Him discerning the true goals for your children and your family.

Are we focused on making our kids look good, which in turn makes us feel successful? Or are we focusing on their hearts? God knows our hearts and our children's hearts, and no test score can override that. We must start with their hearts and ours. We must not be caught up in what others think is success. Our goals come from the Lord and what He has called us to do. We work for an audience of One.

Once we have our goals defined and we are focused on those goals, there is actually freedom. Freedom that we don't have to answer to anyone but the Lord. We know that He will not leave us or forsake us on this journey. That does not mean we won't make mistakes. (Oh boy, do I make so many mistakes on this journey!) Yet God is sovereign and those mistakes will still be used for good. They will be used for us to grow. With our eyes focused on the true goals and what real success is, there is no fear if we make a mistake. We know it is for a purpose.

And we know that in all things God works for the good of those who love him, who have been called according to his purpose.
Romans 8:28

Again, it is helpful to write out your goals. Keep them at the forefront of your mind. Pray over them each day and ask the Lord to help you not forget. Define yourself by success in His eyes, and not the world's eyes.

Chapter 6

WHAT DOES LETTING GOD LEAD LOOK LIKE ON A DAILY BASIS

"The human spirit fails, except where the Holy Spirit fills."
-Corrie ten Boom

Chapter 6
WHAT DOES LETTING GOD LEAD LOOK LIKE ON A DAILY BASIS

"But seek first his kingdom and his righteousness, and all these things will be given to you as well."
Matthew 6:33

When we learn to live out Matthew 6:33, really live it out...we have nothing else to rely on, but Him. We must seek Him first. Not ourselves. Not our plans. When we seek Him first, then His plans become our plans. His will becomes our will.

My will and my plan was to send my children to school. There wasn't even a thought that we would homeschool. Yet here I am, and I can't imagine being anywhere else.

His plan became my plan after a long hard summer of seeking Him, and ultimately surrendering to Him. *Fully.* I prayed, read scripture, and fully focused on Him. I let Him lead, even though it seemed impossible.

God gives us many resources in our lives to use with wisdom and discernment, but not to take the place of Him. We must commit it all to Him first and let Him lead. So often we think we control everything.

As homeschooling moms we do have a big responsibility to our children in educating them. Yet, the problem is when we think that the responsibility solely relies on us. If God called us to do this, He most certainly isn't going to leave us here floundering. He will equip us for every good work. We must claim His words and live these truths.

When we pray for our curriculum choices or how our schooling will look, we do not need to make choices and then ask Him to bless those choices. We do not need to make choices and ask Him to confirm them. No. We need to start simply by praying. Getting close to God. Being in the Word. Spending lots of quiet time with the Lord.

His Word is transforming. The more we fill up on His Word, the more we will be sure we are walking with Him and living out His will. For instance how many times have you decided to use a certain plan for your schooling and then prayed to ask God if it was the right choice? Or did you decide on a co-op and then ask God to bless the choice that you already made?

I say we need to start by being in relationship with Him like no other. Waking up with Him, conversing with him all day and night- that is what praying without ceasing is. It is a relationship with Him, so that your life is in constant union with Him. Being in His Word is not something we "do." It is something we live. We need to let His Word transform us. The Bible says His Word is alive and active. It is powerful. It is not merely a book of rules, instructions or words. It is life. It is life changing. It is transforming.

When we are steeped in the Word, we are transformed. We are filled with His spirit. When we are praying and meditating on the Lord we are filled with His spirit. When we have this type of relationship with the Lord His will becomes our will.

We often want to know what is God's will for my life? Yet, we only have this moment, and God only reveals this moment to us, so perhaps He does not want us to look too far ahead. He wants us to simply seek Him first without conditions and without trying to figure out the future details. He knows the outcome.

Having blind faith ↓ Abraham had it. Heb. 11:8-1D

It all begins with Matthew 6:33. Seek first His righteousness...He *knows* what we need. We do not need to go to Him and ask for what we want, or to bless what we want. We only need to seek Him. By praying. By reading the Word. By living it.

We live by faith, not by Sight. 2Cor. 5:7

When we seek Him first, He will provide for all of our needs, including our homeschools. If we are seeking a relationship with Him above all, we do not need to fear that our needs won't be met. They will be met beyond our expectations.

So change the way you are thinking about your homeschool. Instead of spending countless hours researching the best curricula, styles, and activities, and then praying about which ones to choose, start with just praying. Don't have an agenda in your mind; let God reveal His agenda to you. As you pray and become closer to God, you will understand more clearly what He wants for you.

Spend time with the Lord. How can we have a relationship with someone if we don't spend time with Him? How can we expect to know Him if we don't converse with Him? How can we truly love someone and not stick close to Him?

We are talking about the God who created the universe. Who created you. Who created me. He lifted me straight out of the pit of darkness that I was living in and He rescued me. He placed me into the Light. I am a new creation. Yet, I have the audacity to make excuses for not spending time with Him. I am nothing with out Him. I exist because of Him. My eternity depends on Him. I am being transparent here, because I know that is what I need to do in order to be an encouragement. It is shameful to me, but I know it is too easy to let it happen. I used to make so many excuses. " *I am too tired. I don't have enough time. I am too busy."* ***Oh how that grieves me.***
I had everything backwards. I thought doing everything my way was first, and then I gave my leftover time and attention to God. *"Well, I will pray when I am done with these chores." Or, "I will read my Bible after I check my email."* Yet, then I would want God to still bless all of my efforts. It was

backwards. I wasn't seeking Him first and trusting Him to provide. I was seeking Him *after* I had exhausted all of my own efforts.

How can we even allow those thoughts? Truth is Satan knows we like to be busy bodies. So he tricks us into thinking we are too busy for our God. He tricks us into thinking we can do things in our own strength. He tricks us into putting ourselves above God. Just like in the garden...He deceives. He finds a way to twist the Truth. He makes us think we are too busy for God. Too tired.

Are. You. Kidding. Me.

If I dare say to my God that I am too tired for Him, my faith is dead. My faith depends on Him. Living, breathing, filling up on Him every moment. Without Him, I am dead.

So, that being said, I was convicted. I was ashamed. Since, I have changed my priorities. I don't see my time with the Lord as something to check off my list. I don't see it as something I have to do. You see, the closer you get to God, the more time you want to spend with Him. You can't get enough. You depend on Him for breath. For life.
Yes at times that slithery serpent creeps back in. I slip back, and I put other things above my God. It is a battle. Constantly. Which is why it is so important to recognize the battle and continue to fight the battle.

We need to examine our hearts and our relationship with the Lord. Are we spending time with Him because we want to or because we have to? Are we submitting to Him out of love? Or fear? We need to come to the place where we realize that our everything is dependent on Him, and then, and only then, can we begin to let Him lead us daily...including in our homeschools.

When we make decisions we often get so stuck on the choices. *Is this God's will? Is this the right thing? Is this best for my child?* While we need to be wise and discerning in our decisions, we ultimately have to realize that if we are walking closely with God, we are more likely to be in His will.

I begin each day with the prayer, "Lord help me to teach the children what you want them to learn. Help me to learn what you want me to learn. Give me the strength to do it."

Another way to let the Lord lead is by making the Bible a priority in your family. We don't open a single textbook until we have read the Bible together. There was a time when I would push the Bible aside until math was finished or until our chores were complete. I thought that we would "have time later" after everything else was finished. Again, it's about priorities. What kind of example am I setting for my children, let alone myself, if we don't put Him first? No matter how busy our day is now, we don't do anything until after Bible time. We usually read from a devotional book or some Bible passages, and then sing worship songs together. This sets the tone for the day and aligns our focus on Him.

Then after lunch, before we start up any school again we read the Bible. We pray together, and turn our hearts toward Him. It helps us pray about any situations that have arisen that day and to regroup for the afternoon. Of course we also turn to the Bible during the day whenever the need arises; if we are facing a difficult situation or simply want to offer praise. This year we will be doing even more of an in depth Bible study together as a family. You will read more about that in Chapter 9.

One more very important suggestion is to find other homeschooling friends to pray with. Whether it be daily, weekly, or whatever works for you, it can be transforming. I have a few ladies that have become so dear to my soul because of this. We get together weekly and our kids play, but then we also pray together. This is integral in remembering to let God lead us as homeschoolers.

Chapter 7

COMPARISON TRAP AND EXPECTATIONS

"Spiritual Circumcision: Cutting away everything from life, but the will of God."
-John MacArthur

Chapter 7
COMPARISON TRAP AND EXPECTATIONS

This chapter is something I have talked about often, and will continue to do so because I feel it is such a hindrance in our homeschools. It is the ugly comparison trap; the measuring of our homeschool against others. It needs to stop. It is completely contrary to letting God lead us.

Just like anything in life we often measure ourselves against others. God does not tell us to do this. We are to measure our worth in Him. Our identity is in Him, our value is in Him, and our success is defined by Him. Not others.

The comparison trap is too easy to fall into these days because of the abundance of information on the internet, in magazines, books, etc. It is especially easy to fall into if we are not confident in our homeschool in the first place. If we are in that place where we aren't truly letting God lead us, then we are looking at things in an earthly way. We are defining our success based on other's successes. The truth is what works for someone else may not work for you. Or it may. But that doesn't matter. What matters is, if you have answered the call, and submitted your homeschool to Him. If He is pleased with your efforts, then that is all that matters. God did not call you to homeschool so that your homeschool can look like the neighbor's down the street. Your homeschool is unique to your family. He has determined how your homeschool should look, and if you are letting Him lead you, then you can be assured you are successful. When we rely on what others are doing, it is coveting someone else's life. Once again, we are not relying on Him.

> "Whatever you do, work at it with all your heart,
> as working for the Lord, not for men,"
> **Colossians 3:23**

We tend to look to others because it is so very easy to do so these days. All over the internet are blogs with people's stories and we think they have the perfect family, perfect homeschool, and perfect life. There are two problems with this attitude. First, as sisters in Christ we should rejoice when others are doing good things, and not let the sin of jealousy rear its very ugly head. Second, we should remember that no one is perfect on this earth, and whatever we see is usually the result of "cleaning up" the appearance for all to see. As long as we are being real and authentic it is OK to share the good stuff and the bad stuff.

As a writer I don't want to always write negatively, so more often I share the good lessons I am learning. I don't enjoy wallowing. I don't think it benefits anyone to be a complainer. I want to be edifying. So keep that in mind. The person who is writing has the intention of encouraging the reader, so naturally they will share the good stuff and what is working.

Yet, there has to be a balance so that readers know things aren't always smooth sailing. My most popular post to date was when I published one of our worst weeks ever in our homeschool and titled it, "The Other Side of Homeschool." It was complete with pictures. I felt it was necessary to be encouraging and to see that even in a terrible week, God works. He uses the bad for good. He shapes us through trials. Sharing the struggle is important as long we see that God works through the struggle. So always read with a discerning eye. Look to others for ideas and support, but do not rely on what others are doing or worse what others think. Don't base your worth on what anyone else is doing. As homeschool moms we do ourselves a huge favor when we are truly real and authentic with each other, sharing the ups and downs with the overall goal of supporting each other, lifting each other up and encouraging each other, but not measuring up against each other.

Another trap is when we compare ourselves to others and we set up false expectations for our homeschool. I remember when I was in the "always planning and never doing" stage, and I realized that I was really just living for the expectation, instead of the moment. I wasn't enjoying my homeschool in the present, because I was waiting for what it would be when I had all of my planning complete. God only promises today. Enjoy the moment, and don't live life based on an expectation.

There is so much freedom in homeschooling because we can tailor our children's education to suit their needs. In a school setting there is always comparison. There are standardized tests and peer pressure. At home we are free. We are free to set aside all those hindrances and focus on our unique calling as a family. Don't sabotage that freedom by looking to others. Look to the only one that matters- **God.** Enjoy your freedom as the unique homeschooling family God has created you to be.

Chapter 8

BE PREPARED FOR BAD DAYS

"When though passest through the waters," deep the waves may be and cold, But Jehovah is our refuge, and His promise is our hold; For the Lord Himself hath said, He, the faithful God and true: "When thou comest to the waters, though shalt not go down, but THROUGH."
-Annie Johnson Flint

Chapter 8
BE PREPARED FOR BAD DAYS

We all know the Bible passage about the house built on the sand. We must be building our homeschool based on God as our foundation, so when the storms come we will not be destroyed.

> *"Therefore everyone who hears these words of mine and puts them into practice is like a wise man who built his house on the rock. The rain came down, the streams rose, and the winds blew and beat against that house; yet it did not fall, because it had its foundation on the rock. But everyone who hears these words of mine and does not put them into practice is like a foolish man who built his house on sand. The rain came down, the streams rose, and the winds blew and beat against that house, and it fell with a great crash."*
> **Matthew 77:24-27**

By doing the things laid out in this book- remembering who is in charge, surrendering your homeschool to Him, keeping your eyes on Him, and staying in constant communion with Him, we will be strengthening our foundation. We all know that bad days will come in life and in homeschool, so we must be prepared.

We have so much to do each day, that when we stop and think about all of the tasks we have, we can very quickly get overwhelmed. So we must run on Holy Spirit energy and not on our own strength or intentions.

Expect bad days. Know that the Lord uses everything to grow us. Be prepared by building your foundation on Him and His Word so when times get tough, you will stand strong. Choose to see God's purpose in those days. What can you learn from them?

When your children see that mommy turns to God when things are rough, then you set an example for them to follow as they grow. Where do we turn when things are hard? Turn to Him. Do your children see you praying when there is a tough situation? Do they see you on your knees submitting to His will each day? Point to Him in every situation. Let God lead us, and let our children see that example.

Let Him lead you through the rough waters as well as the calm seas. Trust His plan for it all. I've had so many days where I felt like I could scream (at times I even did!) We all do. Yet it is not OK for us to stay in that place. God promises us we will have troubles in this world. If we didn't, we would have no need to rely on Him.

Isaiah 43:2
When you go through deep waters, I will be with you.

Consider it joy when He uses trials to grow us. We have the opportunity to grow closer to Him through it. Homeschooling is not always easy. Nothing is. Like those missionaries in the jungle, there are challenges. Surrender those days to Him. Prepare yourself by keeping a list of "fighter" verses. Put on that armor of God to prepare you. At the end of this book, there is a list of 31 verses for your homeschool. You can use them for each day of the month to meditate on. They can help you focus each day.

Remember, anytime we are doing something for the glory of God, Satan will try and take us down. So prepare ahead of time. We will experience attack because the enemy hates that we homeschool. We must be prepared for the attacks, and not surprised by them, but welcome them as a chance for our families to grow even closer to God.

I find if I wake up late and do not get into the Word before my children awake it sets me up for a poor heart. My immediate focus is on me and not on Him. *"I need my coffee,"* or *"I'm tired."* I have to fight to wake before my children, but when I do I am much better prepared.

As I wrote in an earlier chapter, we will make mistakes. Expect them. Don't be surprised by them. Rejoice in the fact that God uses them. Do not let mistakes defeat you, rather let them push you to see God's hand in all situations.

Teach your children through mistakes. Let them see how you handle tough times or even decisions that didn't work out as expected. Most of all use them as an opportunity to point them to Him.

If children don't make mistakes they will grow up thinking they will never fail. Failure always produces perseverance. It is OK to fail, as long as we use it for learning and growth. It also helps us to further rely on God. So be prepared for the storms. They will come. Just make sure your foundation is built on the rock.

Chapter 9

USING THE BIBLE AS OUR MAIN TEXT

"Education is useless without the Bible."
-Noah Webster

Chapter 9
USING THE BIBLE AS OUR MAIN TEXT

At the time of this book's publication, I have a new leading from the Lord that I want to share with you for the future of my family's homeschool. It all began with a statement made by Mark Hamby of **Lamplighter Publishing** at a homeschool convention in which he and I were both speaking. He made a statement during one of his presentations that has stuck with me ever since. He stated that if he could do it all over again, he would put away the textbooks for one year and solely study the Bible.

The reason this idea was so appealing to me was that I could only imagine the transformation that would take place in our family if we were in the Bible several hours a day. I wasn't sure how we would do this, but the idea kept coming back to me.

> *Unless the Lord builds the house,*
> *those who build it labor in vain.*
> **Psalm 127:1**

I want our studies to flow from His Word. It is the most important book to know in life. It is where our education starts. I firmly believe God will work an amazing transformation in our family if we devote our studies to His teaching and by always seeking first His righteousness.{Matthew 6:33}

So currently I am working on how all this will look. We are going to go through Genesis, really digging into the Word, breaking it down, and learning. We will also use it for science, geography, and history. We will all work together each morning for however long it takes to truly study the Word. We don't just want to hear it-we want to actively take it in and study it. To know it. To know God.

From there, I have individual work for each child. We will do math and language arts separately, but will also add in other assignments all based on our studies. Copywork will be from scripture. Any research project or language lessons can all be taken from our lessons in the Word, as well as history, science, and geography.

If you visit my website at **Simply Living...for Him**, I have full details of what our studies will look like. Here are some reasons I am excited to start our new Bible study plans:
- **Family centered in the Bible each day.** How can we go wrong if we are all studying God's Word as a family? What an amazing opportunity to grow together as a family.
- **Letting God lead all of our studies.** He IS the best resource we have and the ultimate source of wisdom. He will lead not only our Bible studies, but our academic studies.
- **Activities for all ages.** We will be starting with Genesis and there are so many things we can do for the different age groups. My oldest daughter can delve into the plants and animals created by

God, contrast evolution vs. creation, understand Adam's sin and the fall of man, study the true historical facts of Noah's ark, study ancient maps, and perhaps learn some new Greek words. The younger ones can do these things on their own level.

- **What I can learn.** Learning alongside my children is wonderful. I know God will be teaching me just as much through this process.
- **Discipleship.** Discipleship starts at home. Learning as a family how to truly study the Word is far more important than learning it elsewhere.
- **Following Matthew 6:33.** Truly seeking Him first in all we do, especially in our education is of utmost importance.
- **Giving my children a strong foundation for their spiritual life.** What a beautiful inheritance to gain biblical wisdom!

> *"The boundary lines have fallen for me in pleasant places; surely I have a delightful inheritance"*
> ***Psalm 16:6***

- **Knowing their worth is found in Him.** I want my children to know God. Truly know Him. By knowing Him they will know that their worth only comes from Him. Growing up knowing that truth is a huge goal of mine, especially as I have a daughter entering those oh-so tough middle school years. I don't want them ever to doubt that their identity lies anywhere else but in Him and what He has done.

This is exciting for so many reasons, but most of all... How can I expect us to know God's will, if we don't know God? So, I am following His leading in this and expecting to be transformed.

> "The fear of the LORD is the beginning of knowledge; fools despise wisdom and instruction."
> **Proverbs 1:7**

We must know God above all, and then we will be truly wise.

Chapter 10

Now Let Go And Let Him Lead

"Could there be any more exciting turn in the road than the will of God?"
- Martha Moore, missionary

Chapter 10
Now Let Go And Let Him Lead

As I wrote this book, I prayed diligently. I prayed
for the words that God wanted me to write and for
the ones God wanted to hear those words. I often
laid in my bed each morning thinking about those
who would read this book. I prayed over each of
you, knowing God knows the details.
Only He can be the One to lead you. Only He can be
the One to give you the strength. Only He can be the
One to meet all of your needs.

I pray that before you go one day further in your
journey as a homeschooling family, you put away all
of the "stuff" that has been distracting you. If you
are overwhelmed and gearing up for another year,
stop everything. Stop the planning. Stop the
researching. Stop. Take at least one day, but
preferably several, and go to Him. Plan a "retreat;"
just to commit to praying for your homeschool. Pray
with your husband. Pray as a family. Tell God your
fears. Don't try to find the answers yet. Don't look
for "signs." Don't seek other's advice. He just wants
you to trust, knowing full well that He already has
your needs met.

He's got this.
You don't have to feel confident. You don't have to
be super mom. You merely need to be ready to sit at

His feet and listen. Be like Mary, not Martha.
Remember what Jesus said to Martha :

"Martha, Martha," the Lord answered, "you are
worried and upset about many things, but few
things are needed—or indeed only one. Mary has
chosen what is better, and it will not be taken
away from her."
Luke 10:41-42

When we spend too much time on the details we
miss out on the true teacher in all of this. God. He is
teaching our families. He is in charge. Sit at his feet
awhile and just listen.

Jesus says that Mary had chosen what was better,
and what could not be taken from her. Exactly. The
things Martha was chasing were temporal. They
were details. Earthly things. Mary chose the eternal.
Jesus.

Choose the same for your homeschool. Choose to
chase Him. Not the world.

Go to the Word. Read the scripture and let Him
speak. Don't try to figure out what's ahead. Just be
still. Listen. Embrace His Words. Let Him embrace
you. After you have done these things, rest in Him,
knowing that He is in charge. Seek Him first before
seeking the earthly. Then He will show you what
you are to do on this earth.
So let go, and let Him lead. He knows the outcome.
We only need to trust in His plans. No matter what

they are, He is in control and knows what is best. He will lead you if you simply surrender and listen.

I pray the calling to be a homeschooling family blesses you as you focus on Him, the One who called you..and you will experience the joy that is awaiting you, in being *called home.*

" And let us run with perseverance the race marked out for us, fixing our eyes on Jesus, the pioneer and perfecter of faith."
Hebrews 12:2

Appendix

While seeking First His Righteousness

As homeschooling families, we must cover our homeschools in prayer. It is necessary if we are to succeed. If we seek Him first above all else in our homeschools, we will be on the right path.

Commit to using this guide for 31 days. Read one verse each day. Mediate on it. Pray over it, and see how it applies to homeschool. Read it as a family if you wish. Better yet, write it down somewhere prominent for the whole family to see. Let His Word penetrate the heart of your homeschoool.

We must seek His will diligently each day. Covering our homeschools in prayer will keep our hearts and our homeschools turned toward Him.

If you do this for 31 days, I am hopeful that it will become not just an act for those 31 days, but a lifelong commitment to praying for your homeschool.

As homeschool moms we need to fight off so many battles from the enemey-the world, and sometimes ourselves. Choose today to fight those battles with His Word.

Let God lead your homeschool. We rely never on our own strength, but solely on His.

For more encouragement about simplifying, visit me at my website
www.simplylivingforhim.com

31 Days Of Prayer for Your Homeschool

Day 1
Matthew 6:33
But seek first his kingdom and his righteousness, and all these things will be given to you as well.

Day 2
Philippians 4:8
Finally, brethren, whatever is true, whatever is honorable, whatever is right, whatever is pure, whatever is lovely, whatever is of good repute, if there is any excellence and if anything worthy of praise, dwell on these things.

Day 3
Deuteronomy 6:6-8
These words, which I am commanding you today, shall be on your heart. You shall teach them diligently to your sons and shall talk of them when you sit in your house and when you walk by the way and when you lie down and when you rise up. You shall bind them as a sign on your hand and they shall be as frontals on your forehead. You shall write them on the doorposts of your house and on your gates.

Day 4
Isaiah 54:13

All your sons will be taught by the LORD, and great will be your children's peace.

Day 5
3 John 1:4
I have no greater joy than to hear that my children are walking in the truth.

Day 6
Proverbs 8:17
I love those who love me; And those who diligently seek me will find me.

Day 7
Hebrews 2:13
And again, I will put my trust in him. And again, Behold I and the children which God hath given me.

Day 8
Joshua 24:15
But if serving the LORD seems undesirable to you, then choose for yourselves this day whom you will serve, whether the gods your forefathers served beyond the River, or the gods of the Amorites, in whose land you are living. But as for me and my household, we will serve the LORD.

Day 9
Proverbs 31:15-17
She gets up while it is still dark; she provides food for her family and portions for her servant girls. She consid¬ers a field and buys it; out of her earnings she plants a vineyard. She sets about her work vigorously; her arms are strong for her tasks.

Day 10
Proverbs 22:6

Train up a child in the way he should go, Even when he is old he will not depart from it.

Day 11
Colossians 3:23
Whatever you do, do your work heartily, as for the Lord rather than for men,

Day 12
Matthew 11:28-29
Come to me, all who labor and are heavy laden, and I will give you rest. Take My yoke upon you, and learn of me; for I am gentle and humble in heart, and you will find rest for your souls.

Day 13
Proverbs 3:6
In all your ways submit to him, and he will make your paths straight.

Day 14
Proverbs 3:5
Trust in the LORD with all your heart and lean not on your own understanding;

Day 15
Matthew 6:19
Don't collect for yourselves treasures on earth, where moth and rust destroy and where thieves break in and steal. But collect for yourselves treasures in heaven, where neither moth nor rust destroys, and where thieves don't break in and steal. For where your treasure is, there your heart will be also.

Day 16
Psalm 40: 9-10

I proclaim your saving acts in the great assembly; I do not seal my lips, LORD, as you know.
I do not hide your righteousness in my heart; I speak of your faithfulness and your saving help.
I do not conceal your love and your faithfulness from the great assembly.

Day 17

Exodus 20:1-15

And God spoke all these words, saying, "I am the Lord your God, who brought you out of the land of Egypt, out of the house of slavery. You shall have no other gods before me. You shall not make for yourself a carved image, or any likeness of anything that is in heaven above, or that is in the earth beneath, or that is in the water under the earth. You shall not bow down to them or serve them, for I the Lord your God am a jealous God, visiting the iniquity of the fathers on the children to the third and the fourth generation of those who hate me, ...

Day 18

Romans 12:2

Do not conform any longer to the pattern of this world, but be transformed by the renewing of your mind. Then you will be able to test and approve what God's will is—His good, pleasing and perfect will.

Day 19

1 Corinthians 13:1-13

If I speak in the tongues of men and of angels, but have not love, I am a noisy gong or a clanging cymbal. And if I have prophetic powers, and understand all mysteries and all knowledge, and if I have all faith, so as to remove mountains, but have not love, I am nothing. If I give away all I have, and if I deliver up my body to be burned, but have not love, I gain nothing. Love is patient and kind; love does not envy or boast; it is not arrogant or rude. It does not insist on its own way; it is not irritable or resentful;

Day 20
Psalm 34:17
When the righteous cry for help, the LORD hears and delivers them out of all their troubles.

Day 21
Proverbs 23:12
Commit yourself to instruction; listen carefully to words of knowledge.

Day 22
Philippians 4:13
I can do all things through him who strengthens me.

Day 23
Jeremiah 29:11 For I know the plans I have for you, declares the LORD, plans for welfare and not for evil, to give you a future and a hope.

Day 24
Galatians 5:22-23
But the fruit of the Spirit is love, joy, peace, forbearance, kindness, goodness, faithfulness, gentleness and self-control. Against such things there is no law.

Day 25
Ephesians 6:11-18

Finally, be strong in the Lord and in his mighty power. Put on the full armor of God, so that you can take your stand against the devil's schemes. For our struggle is not against flesh and blood, but against the rulers, against the authorities, against the powers of this dark world and against the spiritual forces of evil in the heavenly realms. Therefore put on the full armor of God, so that when the day of evil comes, you may be able to stand your ground, and after you have done everything, to stand. Stand firm then, with the belt of truth buckled around your waist, with the breastplate of righteousness in place, and with your feet fitted with the readiness that comes from the gospel of peace. In addition to all this, take up the shield of faith, with which you can extinguish all the flaming arrows of the evil one. Take the helmet of salvation and the sword of the Spirit, which is the word of God.

And pray in the Spirit on all occasions with all kinds of prayers and requests. With this in mind, be alert and always keep on praying for all the Lord's people.

Day 26
Psalm 119:66

Teach me good judgment and knowledge, for I believe in your commandments.

Day 27
Proverbs 9:9

Give instruction to a wise man, and he will be still wiser; teach a righteous man, and he will increase in learning.

Day 28
Philippians 4:19
And my God will supply every need of yours according to his riches in glory in Christ Jesus.

Day 29
Ephesians 3:20
Now to him who is able to do immeasurably more than all we ask or imagine, according to his power that is at work within us.

Day 30
Deuteronomy 31:6
Be strong and courageous. Do not fear or be in dread of them, for it is the LORD your God who goes with you. He will not leave you or forsake you.

Day 31
2 Corinthians 4:16-18
So we do not lose heart. Though our outer self is wasting away, our inner self is being renewed day by day. For this light momentary affliction is preparing for us an eternal weight of glory beyond all comparison, as we look not to the things that are seen but to the things that are unseen. For the things that are seen are transient, but the things that are unseen are eternal.

ABOUT THE AUTHOR

Karen DeBeus is a homeschooling mom to four children and is passionate about encouraging homeschooling families. She is the author of Simply Homeschool: Having Less Clutter and More Joy in Your Homeschool, a best seller on Amazon.com. She desires to live more simply so that she can keep her and her family's focus on Jesus. She has been brought to her knees many times by the grace God has given her, and she writes about her journey to simplify all areas of her life at her blog Simply Living...for Him.

Karen loves to connect with others through her speaking and writing. She can be reached at karen@simplylivingforhim.com

© Simply Living...For Him 2012

www.SimplyLivingforHim.com

BOOK DESIGN AND PUBLISHED BY
FARMHAUS STUDIOS

Made in the USA
Lexington, KY
02 March 2016